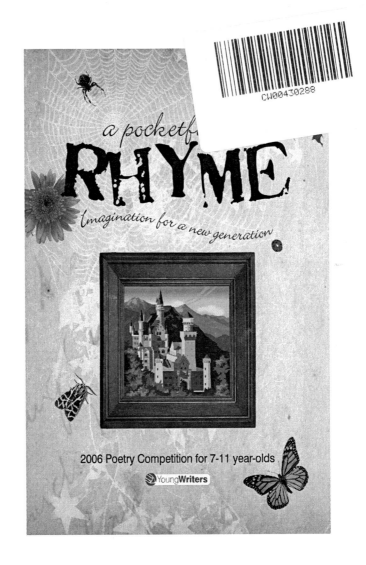

a pocketf...

RHYME

Imagination for a new generation

2006 Poetry Competition for 7-11 year-olds

Young**Writers**

South Yorkshire

Edited by Claire Tupholme

 Young**Writers**

First published in Great Britain in 2006 by:
Young Writers
Remus House
Coltsfoot Drive
Peterborough
PE2 9JX
Telephone: 01733 890066
Website: www.youngwriters.co.uk

SB ISBN 1 84602 573 7

Foreword

Young Writers was established in 1991 and has been passionately devoted to the promotion of reading and writing in children and young adults ever since. The quest continues today. Young Writers remains as committed to the nurturing of poetic and literary talent as ever.

This year's Young Writers competition has proven as vibrant and dynamic as ever and we are delighted to present a showcase of the best poetry from across the UK and in some cases overseas. Each poem has been selected from a wealth of *A Pocketful Of Rhyme* entries before ultimately being published in this, our fourteenth primary school poetry series.

Once again, we have been supremely impressed by the overall quality of the entries we have received. The imagination, energy and creativity which has gone into each young writer's entry made choosing the poems a challenging and often difficult but ultimately hugely rewarding task - the general high standard of the work submitted ensured this opportunity to bring their poetry to a larger appreciative audience.

We sincerely hope you are pleased with this final collection and that you will enjoy *A Pocketful Of Rhyme South Yorkshire* for many years to come.

Contents

Abbie Simmons (10)   37
Kadee Leigh Bills (11)   38
Faye Mayfield (11)   39
Brendan Simpson (10)   40
Daniel Pearce (11)   41
Macauley Wilson (10)   42
Katie Barrett (11)   43
Andrew Lacey (11)   44
Ellen Capel (11)   45
Cassidy Cotz (10)   46
Emily Noonan (10)   47
Hayley Woodward (11)   48
Lyndon Staniland (10)   49
Bradley Wilson (9)   50
Conner Ramsay (9)   51
Bethany Hudson (9)   52
Kay Hartley (9)   53
Ryan Wigley (9)   54
Connor Sykes (9)   55
Byron Hughes (9)   56
Liam Hoyland (8)   57
Kerri Walker (9)   58
Georgina Crookes (9)   59
Alex Walker (8)   60
Sally Hampshire (9)   61

Hill Top Primary School
Jemma Taylor (11)   62
Damon Brown (11)   63
Kathryn Ackroyd (11)   64
Aidan Little (11)   65
Samantha Fretwell (11)   66
Amy Holland (11)   67
Jack Hewitt (11)   68
Shannon Reid (11)   69
Katy Goodwin (11)   70
Kayleigh Ferguson (11)   71
William Dunkerley (10)   72
Thomas Madine (11)   73
Lewis Clarke (11)   74
Robyn Cusworth (11)   75

Amy Townshend (11)   76
Rebecca Willoughby (11)   77
Lauren Wakelin (10)   78
Rebecca Bagley (10)   79

Loxley Primary School

Thomas Oakes (8)   80
Charlotte Bye (8)   81
Megan Walker (9)   82
Natasha Moran (8)   83
Iona McLeod (8)   84
Cameron East (9)   85
Jasmine Blocksidge (9)   86
Rebecca Weston (9)   87
Molly Smith (9)   88
Harvey Hancock (9)   89
Briony Davis (9)   90
Jennifer Knowles (9)   91
Jack Sampson (8)   92
Samuel Turner (8)   93
Kieran Quick (9)   94
Jake Chorlton (9)   95
Sophie Barnsley (9)   96
Mark Raw (9)   97

St Marie's Catholic Primary School, Sheffield

Ben Sproston (8)   98
Michelle Maora (8)   99
Tyler Simmonite-Scott (8)   100
Paris Dephley (9)   101
Dominic Casey (9)   102
Jack Clohessy (9)   103
John Rossiter (9)   104
Ophelia Phillips (8)   105
Ian Mercado (9)   106
Sophie Farrell (10)   107
Alex Kilcommons (9)   108
Fadzai Chitunhu (9)   109
Katherine Stent (10)   110
Owen Creaser-Smith (10)   111
Chinyere Clarke (10)   112

Kyle Taylor (10)   152
Bethany Wood (9)   153
Alex Joburns (10)   154
Rose Whitelam (10)   155
Elizabeth Wignall (8)   156
Holly Lockwood (9)   157
Tabitha Finnerty (8)   158
Corey Daley (9)   159
Kelly Gregory (10)   160
Hannah Barker (10)   161
Molly Lee (8)   162
Becky Hirst (9)   163
Haydn Brownsword (9)   164
Danny Hibbert (10)   165

Totley All Saints CE (VA) Primary School
Daisy Hope (8)   166
Emmy Beeby (8)   167
Katie Harvey (7)   168
Mia Wilson (7)   169
Megan Jones (8)   170
Sam Smith (7)   171
Emily Hulme (8)   172
Libby Honnor (8)   173

Westways Primary School
Sanaa Ghori (11)   174
Hannah James-Louwerse (11)   175
Hannah Grafton (11)   176
Loma Al-Dahiyat (10)   177
Isaac Proudfoot (11)   178
Meg Plowright (10)   179
Joëlle Brabban (11)   180
Rory Hanna (10)   181
Woo-Jeong Yoon (11)   182
Rowan Drury (10)   183

The Poems

Africa - Haikus

Elephants are huge
Crocodiles snap their big mouths
Penguins being fed

Tortoises moving
My music makes me happy
Giraffes eating leaves.

Alyx Walker (8)
Aston Hall J&I School

Countryside

I see . . .
The barley blowing in the air
With the country breeze in my face
And the smooth smell, lovely and fresh.
I see . . .
Hay and tractors, fresh as anything
And the beautiful crops
Growing with the fantastic, strong, green trees.
I see . . .
The brilliant dandelions shifting from side to side
And the huge fields opening up from winter
And my wellingtons sludging in the mud.
I see . . .
The spiky hedges blocking the view
With the rocky paths with stepping footsteps
And the dead dandelions telling the time.

Tyler Snelling (9)
Aston Hall J&I School

The Magic Box

(Based on 'Magic Box' by Kit Wright)

I will put in the box . . .
My fantastic Indiana Jones game
'Goonie's R Good Enough' music
The splash of the swimming pool.

I will put in the box . . .
The swing of a gorilla swinging through the trees
The taste of chocolate cake
The goodness of 'The Goonies' film.

I will put in the box . . .
The blueness of a blue whale flapping through the waves
The hitting of my Kong toys
The funniness of my friends.

Liam Thornhill (8)
Aston Hall J&I School

The Magic Box

(Based on 'Magic Box' by Kit Wright)

I will put in my magic box . . .
Oozing, lovely, hard, melting chocolate
Fun, enjoyable and relaxing times
Goes on forever Monopoly

I will put in my magic box . . .
Daring, stupid, funny Tracy Beaker book
Cute, furry, brown, black, funny pup
Healthy, enjoyable Sunday dinner.

I will put in my magic box . . .
Screaming, crazy, lively people
Unlucky for some, a 13th month
Bright, amazing orange.

I will put in my magic box . . .
Relaxing, calm, enjoying myself
A smooth boat ride
Colourful, gold, small box.

Chloe Murdoch (9)
Aston Hall J&I School

I Will Put In My Box . . .

(Based on 'Magic Box' by Kit Wright)

I will put in my box . . .

Horses galloping and neighing across the grass,
Tasty, cheesy, stringy spaghetti,
Splashing, swimming, jumping dolphins as soft as silk,
And more.

I will put in my box . . .

My best friends Chloe, Gemma and Chloe M,
The funniest clowns in the world,
I will put in all the Jacqueline Wilson books,
And more.

I will put in my box . . .

12 days in a week,
A baby's first smile,
A TV with a thousand channels,
And more.

My box is in the shape of an ice cream,
It has glossy pink ice cream
And a chocolate cornet,
And I'll keep it forever!

Hannah O'Kane (9)
Aston Hall J&I School

My Magic Box

(Inspired by 'Magic Box' by Kit Wright)

I will go in my box with . . .

A massive Shire horse
A tasty, snacky cheeseburger
And a Lamborghini that roars

I will go in my box with . . .

A right long game of cricket that's fun
The sky that's as blue as the sea below
And Fluffy shall not die with a gun.

Joshua Parkin (8)
Aston Hall J&I School

The Magic Shopping Trolley

(Inspired by 'Magic Box' by Kit Wright)

I will put in my shopping trolley . . .

A show-jumping monster jumping over me
The skin of a dead snake lying on my feet
A guinea pig squealing for her food.

I will put in my shopping trolley . . .

The scorching hot Spanish sun shining to the top
The African music running through my ears
The Scottish dancing tapping through my head.

I will put in my shopping trolley . . .

The witches pulling their faces out of the book
My portrait up on the gleaming white wall
The smoke coming from the BBQ stall.

I will put in my shopping trolley
Kelly Clarkson's voice moving through my ears.

Leanne Smith (9)
Aston Hall J&I School

The Magic Box

(Based on 'Magic Box' by Kit Wright)

I will put in my box . . .

An ice cream that melts in the sun
And cools me down in the summer.
Anfield - the roar of the crowd
After seeing Liverpool scoring a goal.

I will put in my box . . .

The blood drop of a stormy Norman
Finishing the battle in 1066.
Triple H doing the Pedigree on Eage
To win the WWE championship.
The Rooney goal of the season.

I will put in my box . . .

The football league season of Sheffield United
Going to the Premiership!

Sam Drury (8)
Aston Hall J&I School

Africa - Haikus

Safari giraffes,
The beat of the drum,
Safari lions.

Snappy crocodiles,
Elephants are beautiful,
They're my favourite.

Hippos really fat,
Iguanas invisible,
Giraffes eating leaves.

Jackolopes bouncing,
Tortoises moving slowly,
Music makes you dance.

Gemma Hunt (8)
Aston Hall J&I School

The Magic Box

(Based on 'Magic Box' by Kit Wright)

In my box I will put . . .

The shiny waters blue
My favourite football highlights of my team
An aeroplane flying over England

I will put into my box . . .

Delicious Cadbury's chocolate melting in my mouth
A leopard running across an enclosure at 60mph
My favourite book reading itself out to me

In my box I will put . . .

A PS2 with TV included
An ice rink with super slippy ice
A TV programme with mystery to be solved

I will put into my box . . .

A train with a TV on each seat
My favourite PS2 game with all-new technology
A hang-glider as big as an elephant

In my box I will put . . .

An ice cream fresh from the freezer
A warm day in Portugal
A cool day in Lapland.

Laurence Machin (9)
Aston Hall J&I School

Crocodiles - Haiku

Crocs are hideous
Crocodiles are so monstrous
Their teeth are chainsaws.

Mitchell Redfearn (8)
Aston Hall J&I School

Playtime - Haiku

Everyone dancing
Playing tig around the tree
People going mad.

Damon Coulson (9)
Aston Hall J&I School

Magic Box

(Based on 'Magic Box' by Kit Wright)

I will put in the box . . .
The star of a million skies
The fur of a running dog
And the cute face of a hamster.

I will put in the box . . .
A smell of spag Bol
The grass of the garden
And the three moons.

Daniel McVeigh (9)
Aston Hall J&I School

Fille The Special Box

I will put in Fille . . .
The sweet and salt from a giant popcorn
The mouth-watering taste of the lolly
And the seeds from the fruit that's mistaken for a vegetable -
The tomato.

I will put in Fille . . .
The fur from the giant itself, Big Foot
The chattering and chopping jaws of the great white shark
And the spirit from my great, great grandma.

I will put in Fille . . .
The mysterious place under the ocean - Atlantic Ocean
A little cyber world from the future
And the crown from King Henry VIII.

Fille box has stars and gold in the corners
And a tornado in the middle of it.
Fille is the same size as a mouse.

Cameron Lewis (9)
Aston Hall J&I School

My Magic Shopping Trolley

(Inspired by 'Magic Box' by Kit Wright)

I will put in the trolley . . .
A pizza covered in cheese
A melting chocolate bar
Ice cream covered in toffee sauce.

I will put in my trolley . . .
A cat, badly fluffy
36 hours in a day
A game of hard Cluedo.

I will put in my trolley . . .
A flight on Virgin
Annoying people, fun
Candyfloss all tasty.

Something as clear as glass
I'd put in the trolley clear, pure water.

My trolley is clear, pure glass - gold and silver ice-cold paint
I shall keep this trolley forever.

Chloe Rumboll (9)
Aston Hall J&I School

Food

Food is the first thing on my mind
And if you offer it to me,
I will be kind.
Friends and family tell me to go on a diet,
But I will cause a riot.
People most give me food
And that is why I eat so rude.

Corie Jackman (11)
Beck Primary School

Birthday Beats

It's my birthday once again,
I'm ready for school
And I look cool.
I'm sitting in the classroom,
I think I need the bathroom,
It's birthday time to tell.

It's playtime already
And I need to be steady,
Because of the birthday beats.
Oh no!

Nicola Tibbs (10)
Beck Primary School

The Monkey In The Garden

The monkey in the garden
He makes a scene
If his trees aren't very clean
He gets his own way
By crying all day.

If his mate breaks his heart
He will tear the trees apart
His favourite food is cooked koala
He's never touched a banana.

Once he fell with a clump
And threw himself in the dump
The monkey had a gang
But they threw him out with a big bang.

Kayden Wiggan (10)
Beck Primary School

Untitled

Football, ice hockey,
I like ice hockey the most
Because I love ice.

Ice hockey I like the most,
Because I know the Steelers.

Steelers, I love them the most,
Because I love Gavin Farrand and Mike Peron.

Jade Riley (8)
Beck Primary School

I've Got A Friend

I've got a friend, her name is Jade,
She's so cute and she always goes to Spain.

I've got a friend, her name is Jenna,
She always moans about the weather.

I've got a friend, her name is Hayley,
When she gets picked on, she tells Miss Bayley.

I've got a friend, her name is Lauren,
When she does the water bottles, she wets her bottom.

I've got a friend, her name is Megan,
She thinks she'll go to Heaven.

I've got a friend, her name is Laura,
She goes out to play with her dog Lea.

I've got a friend, her name is Wednesday,
She's got a baby brother called Mackenzie.

Carmen Crookes (9)
Beck Primary School

Drip, Drop, Drip

Drip, drop, drip, I'm dripping from a tap,
Drip, drop, drip, I'm falling on a mat,
Drip, drop, drip, I'm really wet,
Drip, drop, drip, I'm a little thing.
The force I push in the tap,
It hurts and it's really loud,
Drip, drop, drip, I'm squashed on the ground.

Hayley German (9)
Beck Primary School

The Trick That Went Wrong

I was really out of breath,
But I'd still much running to do,
Because someone was chasing me,
The school bully and his crew.

Then a figure came along,
Dressed in a white sheet,
Coming just behind him,
The policeman on his beat.

It was my best friend,
Acting as a ghost,
To be very honest,
PC Green was scared the most.

Then an idea popped into my mind,
So I asked my friend for help,
He agreed it would be funny,
To see the school bully yelp.

So my friend, as a ghost, scared the bully,
But the great coward had a knife,
When he jumped, it slid across the ghost's neck . . .
And cut the cords of my friend's life.

But his death was not too sad,
Worthwhile was his pain,
For the bully went on holiday
And never came back again.

Gregor Smith (11)
Beck Primary School

A Friend Poem

Do you have a friend?
I have a friend.

Her eyes gleam like stars,
But look like chocolate bars.

We play with her bouncy ball,
But as she catches it, she bangs on the wall.

She has a cat,
That kills rats.

She has blonde hair,
She wouldn't cut it because she wouldn't dare
And her head would go bare!

Wednesday Quinones (9)
Beck Primary School

My Mad Family

My family is so mad, they can hardly speak to each other.
They have to use a pad to ask each other questions.
They're so mad, they smash everything up.
I am not mad, it is just them.
I've even told them I am going to live with my friend Jade Hope Riley.
Jade has got a really big house.
She has got a 5-bedroomed house.

Megan Farnell (9)
Beck Primary School

Fun Bun

My dad will get me a job as a clown,
When I do it I will wear a crown,
A funny wig, orange and big.

I will start my job today,
My boss says I need a name,
It should be good and not glum,
I know! My name will be Fun Bun.

All I need are baggy trousers,
Big enough to cover houses,
I need a big red nose,
Clumpy shoes, hope they don't bruise!

I have got to go,
Hope you enjoy the show!

Bradley Vaughan (9)
Beck Primary School

Bratz

Bratz, they always have to dress the best,
Making fashion shows without a rest,
Jade's on the go without messing around,
Yasmin has got on the old, silly frown,
Sasha in the background organising her make-up,
Chloe's got her hands full with her best make-up,
With Chloe on the go and Jade messing around,
They can't find the message that Sasha just found.

Jenna Barnes (9)
Beck Primary School

Real Pain

My mum is a real pain,
When I am bad she whacks me with a cane.

When I am good she spoils me insane,
When I am really bad she picks me up with a crane
And ties me to a train.

Shane Newsam (9)
Beck Primary School

Sweets

Sweets, sweets
All around
Every shop
Anywhere.
Looking all around the house
Must have sweets
Must be found.

Round and round
The house I searched
The sweets could not
Be found.

Sweets are good
Sweets are great
But don't eat too many
Or you will be *sick!*

Kirsty Wilson (10)
Beck Primary School

Man City Football Club

Man City football club have their ups and downs,
But then there is their manager who always acts a clown.
Then, oh my gosh, look at the ball flying
Into the back of the Man City goal.
Now that's the end of the Man City game
And all the players can hang their heads in shame.

Oliver Flint (11)
Beck Primary School

The SATs

SATs are like rats with hats
Every single day SATs are boring
I wish I could just go to Dover
It's like they're sucking your brain like a Hoover.

I'm glad that SATs are only for a week
SATs are like bats in darkness
We work all year to do the SATs
We hear the teacher talking all the time.

SATs are just boring every year
I wish I could just relax and have a beer
There's only three subjects in the SATs
All the teachers are like cats.

Bradley Robinson (11)
Beck Primary School

Poem

One day I was kicking a football about
Knocked over a vase and a genie popped out.
'You have three wishes, but it best not be kisses.'

One day after school, I went in my pool,
I sat by the fire and I think I got higher.

My sister thinks Nan is fun,
I don't because I prefer to run.
Ahhhhh!

Ryan Pearson (11)
Beck Primary School

Pets

Pets are just pets
They put you in debts
Some live in nets
And drink when it's wet

Pets bite you when it's tight
But still they eat your inside up
Pets eat all day long
And sleep all night long

Pets help you, but when they die
You feel all sad inside
Keep them safe, happy and warm
Then they'll enjoy their life so long.

Alice Whaley (11)
Beck Primary School

My School Day

Wake up early in the morning
All my bones are groaning
Get dressed quick
I'm nearly sick.

Speed-walk to school
See little kids drool
First lesson, maths
Not a bundle of laughs.

Afternoon is fun
In the sun
Yay! I can go home and play out
Or maybe I might stay in and lounge about.

Lauren Holmes (11)
Beck Primary School

Wet Lunchtime

Wet lunchtime is boring for me
And sometimes, somehow
Makes me think of a jubilee.
Next thing you know
Your class has got the award
And then something will happen
And it will be about a person on board.

The boring thing about wet lunchtime
Is the sky is always grey
And there is nothing to do
But somehow play.
The weird thing about wet lunchtime is
That you somehow have fun
In fact I'd rather have a muffin bun.

You rush to school
To see that sunshine on the field
But all you see is wet grass
You just want to yield.
At the end of the day
The sunshine comes
And the rain drains.

Daniel Smith (10)
Beck Primary School

Vehicles

Cars are fast
Cars are slow
Cars are a blast
Cars can be low.

Vans are big
Like a pig
Vans are tall
Like a wall.

Buses are long
That's nothing wrong
Buses are fun
As eating a bun.

Trains are fast
And they're good fun
You'll have a blast
You won't get done.

Jack Beal (11)
Beck Primary School

Poems Of Rhymes

Transport can be fast,
Even from the past,
You can be made into a toad,
If you drive a Ford.

Can you read hard books?
Can you play hockey with hard pucks?
Can you make noises like ducks?
Can you even make hucks?

I'm eleven, not seven,
I'm as tall as a tree, not a bee,
My legs are very short, as short as a boat,
My arms are very small, like a ball.

Bradley Moffatt (11)
Beck Primary School

My Dad

My dad loves his chair
He will do anything to comb his hair
My dad loves his chocolate mushed with pear
When my dad gets up he will lounge in his chair
My dad is brilliant because he is Dad with his chair.

Abbie Simmons (10)
Beck Primary School

SATs Are Over

SATs were quite hard
But at least I got a good luck card
When I finished I felt like a lump of lard.

I hate SATs
And that is that
And nobody can change it.

Finally, SATs are over
It was just like driving a rusty Rover
But at least now they are actually over.

Kadee Leigh Bills (11)
Beck Primary School

SATs

SATs are all in a big hat
They fly away like a bat
Some questions easy
In fact they're easy peasy.

You do them in every school
You don't do them in Year one
Because they're only babies
And don't know what to do.

In Year 6 you do your big ones
They're not easy
After them you'll feel very wheezy
And a bit queasy.

So don't go near anybody who's done their SATs
Because they might be feeling a bit wheezy and a bit queasy.

Faye Mayfield (11)
Beck Primary School

Fast Cars

Some cars are fast, some cars are slow,
Some cars are even like lightning.
Some cars are small, some cars are big,
Some cars are done up, some cars are boring.
Some cars race, some cars don't,
Some cars are nice, some cars aren't.
Some cars can be like jeeps, some cars are like coaches,
Some are like vans, some are like lorries.
All F1 cars race around a track,
Whereas normal cars are driving on roads.
Some rally cars go on dirt tracks ten times, ten laps,
Cars can be big or small or medium sizes.

Brendan Simpson (10)
Beck Primary School

Six Week Holidays

Leaving school is so cool
Holidays on the beach
There's so much to do
Give yourself a treat!

Going to the arcade
Doing something wrong
People blaming me
I get grounded for so long!

Daniel Pearce (11)
Beck Primary School

Six Weeks

Leaving school is so cool,
I like playing in my swimming pool,
Watching TV all day long,
Playing football in the park,
Tricking all the players with my skill
That everyone fears.

Going home to have my tea,
Staying up late on my PSP,
That's how to spend a holiday.

Eating crisps and chocolate
Is being greedy,
But I can't help it,
It's just so delicious.
But then I think about secondary school.
Nooooo!

Macauley Wilson (10)
Beck Primary School

Best Friends

My best friend is so cool,
She never behaves like a fool.
They say you can have more than one best friend,
But they may drive you round the bend.
Best friends are there when you need them,
Best friends are as precious as a gem.

Katie Barrett (11)
Beck Primary School

Fast Cars

Zooming down the motorway really fast,
We're going 100mph at last.
Until I've got whiplash, which is bad,
We went to hospital and my dad was really sad.

Andrew Lacey (11)
Beck Primary School

Together

Mates all laughing and joking
You're all very doting.
We're all together forever
We'll never forget each other, never!
Our class united
All so very excited!
We stick together no matter what
Even if it means landing on our tot!
We're all together forever
We stick together like a bird to a feather!

Ellen Capel (11)
Beck Primary School

I Scored A Goal

I scored a goal today
I felt like saying, 'Yay!'
When the ball hit the net
It was the day I couldn't forget.
My mum was so surprised
On the day she opened her eyes.
I had a blast
Even though our team came last.
But my mum was cold
That's what I was told.
Shivering on the line
Until penalty time.
I took a chance
For our team's advance.

Football mad me!

Cassidy Cotz (10)
Beck Primary School

Leaving Friends

Leaving friends behind
It's so unkind.
It's time to say
Today's the day.
We scream goodbye
Our smiles are high.

My mates are cool
We hang in the pool.
Sometimes we act like a fool
Next time it's secondary school!
Ahhh!

Emily Noonan (10)
Beck Primary School

Shopaholic

Shopping at Meadowhall,
Shopping anywhere,
Shopping down town,
I don't really care!

As long as I get all my stuff,
As long as I don't miss the bus,
As long as I get my ear muffs
And as long as the police don't have to cuff.
I'm off!

Hayley Woodward (11)
Beck Primary School

Being A Teenager

When I am a teenager I want to be like my big brother,
Driving a Ferrari, neons glowing, window tint shining.
Nos squeaking and petrol burning like hell, BBS alloys,
Because I am going to be like my big brother - sharp and smart.

Lyndon Staniland (10)
Beck Primary School

Alliteration

One ostrich eating oranges
Two tigers talking to themselves
Three thin turtles taking a trophy
Four flying fish flying past
Five fat friends fighting for fish fingers
Six seagulls swooping slowly
Seven spiders spinning a web
Eight elephants eating Easter eggs
Nine nice nannies knitting
Ten talking teddy bears telling tales.

Bradley Wilson (9)
Beck Primary School

Things I'd Do If It Wasn't For My Teacher

Pretend to be King Kong,
Stick out my tongue,
Do no work,
Go berserk,
Bounce on tables,
Rip up fables,
Arrive late,
Avoid my fate,
Stick people's heads down the loo,
Wear a tutu,
Spit paper at the walls,
While the attendance falls.

Conner Ramsay (9)
Beck Primary School

Plip Plop - A Water Haiku

Plip plop bubbles pop
Tea towels get very wet
Plip plop bubbles pop.

Bethany Hudson (9)
Beck Primary School

Water - Haikus

At bath time I have
Difficulty getting my
Toe out of the tap.

Near my garden I
Have a little waterfall
Which I think is great.

Kay Hartley (9)
Beck Primary School

Spring

S pring has finally sprung
P etunias sprouting out
R abbits peering out of dens
I rises growing like mad
N ight falls very late
G inger cats purring like a Ferrari.

Ryan Wigley (9)
Beck Primary School

Spring

S ea gets warmer
P lants and trees grow
R abbits hop
I see chicks and ducks
N o more snow
G inger cats purring.

Connor Sykes (9)
Beck Primary School

Spring

S pring, the sun starts to shine
P lay out until later
R abbits are out in the sun
I n a field there are horses
N est full of birds
G alaxy in the sun.

Byron Hughes (9)
Beck Primary School

Spring

S inging birds and rabbits making nests
P urple lavender making the world smell nice
R abbits hopping in the meadow
I ce can no longer be seen
N ests with baby chicks inside
G inger cats purring like a Ferrari.

Liam Hoyland (8)
Beck Primary School

Spring

S unflowers getting ready to bud
P lants getting planted in a tub
R ainbow appears to be going away
I ce cream coming all the time
N ever going to be freezing this season
G reen, glossy, golden grass.

Kerri Walker (9)
Beck Primary School

Spring

S pringtime makes eggs crack
P ink roses coming out to sing
R ainbow shining bright over the hills
 I ce melting that people skate beautifully on
N ests with baby birds in them
G oing to be summer soon.

Georgina Crookes (9)
Beck Primary School

Spring

S inging birds across the land
P ink pigs snorting in their sleep
R oses rising in the light
I ce is melting in the rivers
N ew birds, lambs and chicks are born
G orgeous sunflowers in the sun.

Alex Walker (8)
Beck Primary School

Spring

S parkling daffodils in the meadow
P recious red roses growing in the soil
R abbits jumping all around us
I can see lots of beautiful flowers
N ew baby animals born everywhere
G rowing plants all gathered together.

Sally Hampshire (9)
Beck Primary School

Love

Love is pink and red like roses holding my heart together,
Love is something that you think of forever and ever.

Love is help that chases away all your fears,
Love is care and feelings that take back all those little tears.

Love is warmth that travels around our body,
When we have no love it makes our day unusually foggy.

Love reminds me of raindrops meandering down a rose petal,
Love is like a boiling, steaming kettle.

Love tastes like a sweet and sour meal,
Love is something different and superior that you feel.

Love is powerful and nothing compares,
Love is something that everyone shares.

Jemma Taylor (11)
Hill Top Primary School

Anger

Anger is red like a volcano ready to explode.
Anger is like a gun voraciously shooting.
Anger reminds me of when I fall out with my friends.
Anger is jealousy and rage inside us.
Anger feels like a devil living inside me telling me to do something
that I should not do.
It feels like I just want to cry and do nothing at all.
Anger smells like hot chilli peppers waiting to burn people's thoughts.
Anger makes me feel like I want to kick a ball furiously.
Anger sounds like a car screeching, full of rage, ready to crash.

Damon Brown (11)
Hill Top Primary School

Anger!

Anger is red, like a violent, exploding volcano,
while down below people running and screaming, trying to get away.
Anger tastes like red-hot tomato soup slithering smoothly
down your throat.
Anger reminds me of a devil living inside me, telling me to do things
I shouldn't.
Anger looks like an angry fire burning its way through
an innocent house.
Anger sounds like a small, poor boy crying for help, while bullies
beat him up.
Anger feels like big, sharp, pointy spikes ready to spike you.
Most of all, anger is red.

Kathryn Ackroyd (11)
Hill Top Primary School

Silence

Silence is like great thick snow,
Filling up all the spaces that you know.

Silence feels like loneliness,
With happiness getting less and less.

Silence reminds you of being glad,
Something that you always had.

Silence smells like smoke,
Finally disappearing and giving you hope.

Silence sounds like heavy metal
And standing on a stinging nettle!

Silence is something we have to have
And have to live with.

Aidan Little (11)
Hill Top Primary School

Love Beat

Love is bright pink like a bunch of flowers,
Love is the thing that gives you all the powers.

Love is as hot as the sun,
Love is with a partner then makes your heart weigh a ton.

Love smells like a box of melted treats,
Love is the thing that makes my heart beat.

Love tastes like a big red heart with my blood,
I would do anything for love if I could.

Love feels like a big bear hug,
Love travels like a bug.

Love sounds like a romantic night,
When I think of love, I never think of fright.

Love is like a big pot of gold,
Love is hot, not even nearly cold.

Love is what I need to carry on.

Samantha Fretwell (11)
Hill Top Primary School

Fear Poem

Fear is black,
Like you're trapped in a dark, hollow hole
And nobody knows you're there.

Fear tastes like medicine dripping down your throat,
You're trying to cough it up
But it's already gone down.

Fear smells like burning coal,
Wafting it away frantically,
But it's going up your nose.

Fear looks like the stormy sea,
Crashing against the flinty,
Dull, black rocks.

Fear reminds me of something I've never seen before,
But I can feel it in my bones,
It's like a devil in my body, controlling my soul.

Amy Holland (11)
Hill Top Primary School

Love

Love is like a red waterfall gushing in the valley.
It tastes like melted chocolate trickling down my throat.
It smells like a rose blooming in the field.
Love feels like a cuddly teddy wanting you to cuddle it.

Jack Hewitt (11)
Hill Top Primary School

Love

Every time I think of you I go cold
I look at you as a pot of gold
I think of you, how you are so bold.

You broke my heart
Now we are apart
You threw a dart.

I thought I was the best
But suddenly you left
And you needed a rest.

If you are in a mess
Call me SOS
So come and bless.

I feel like a ball on fire
There's something about you that I admire
You wrap round me like a piece of wire.

Shannon Reid (11)
Hill Top Primary School

Anger

Anger is like a ferocious dragon
Lurking over the deserted town.

Anger sounds like a raging, purple roller coaster cart
Across the metal tracks.

Anger smells like a giant rock pool of lava
Swirling around the irregular shaped rocks.

Anger feels like a silver sword
Ripping through your heart in a bloody battle.

Anger looks like a red parcel
With a time bomb ticking away . . . and away.

Katy Goodwin (11)
Hill Top Primary School

Love

Love is very happy,
Not like anger which makes us snappy.

Love is red,
Like a sweet, romantic song.

Love tastes like pure lemons,
Resting on your tongue.

Love sounds like wedding bells,
Ringing in your heart.

Love feels soft,
Like a huge teddy hugging you tight.

Love looks like a box of chocolates,
Melting down your throat.

Love reminds me of
Two people loving each other with all their hearts forever.

Love is like a parcel,
Delivered to your door.

Love is like a time bomb,
Ticking for evermore.

Kayleigh Ferguson (11)
Hill Top Primary School

Darkness

Darkness is black like a vortex into space
Darkness smells like a factory on New Year's Eve
Darkness feels cold like the Antarctic at its coldest temperature
Darkness tastes like eating a big bowl of ice cubes getting
                                rammed down someone's throat
Darkness looks like an abandoned mine with rats screeching
Darkness reminds me of people scratching on the blackboard.

William Dunkerley (10)
Hill Top Primary School

Darkness

Darkness is black like a storm cloud gathering for an attack.
Darkness reminds me of a black dog lurking behind a tree,
waiting to pounce.
Darkness smells like rotten egg and dead fish.
Darkness looks like a dragon watching you wherever you go.
Darkness tastes like slime-covered, burnt toast.
Darkness sounds quiet and loud!
Darkness feels smooth, but it's deadly!

Thomas Madine (11)
Hill Top Primary School

Silence And Fear

Silence leads to death
Death leads to anger
Anger leads to fear
Fear rises above everything
The colour of fear is misty and cold.

I am here, silent not a squeak!
I can run like the wind
Spring so fast, you won't even see me fly
What am I?

I can fight with fire
What could I be?
There is a lot more than you think
So hard, breathing fire like a goblet
I can eat humans
What could I be?

Lewis Clarke (11)
Hill Top Primary School

Love Is Like . . .

Love is like desired red, scarlet, rich and pure,
Love is like a link, every one endures.

Love is like butterflies fluttering in a heart,
Love is between two people not to tear apart.

Love is strong, unstopping, overpowering everything,
Love is like a sunny meadow in the time of spring.

Love is like a passion flower flowing in a breeze,
Love is like a yellow, honey, buzzy bumblebee.

Love tastes like expensive chocolate, melting on a tongue,
Love is like a violin playing a heartfelt song.

Love is like the sunset sun with the golden sky,
Love is like a warming tear not to release or cry.

Love is like a ripe pink balloon floating into space,
Love is a main character in the human race.

Love is powerful, romantic, passionate and very sweet,
Love is something that in the future you will meet!

Robyn Cusworth (11)
Hill Top Primary School

Sadness

Sadness is grey like a lonely old man waiting for death to come.
Sadness tastes like a teardrop rolling down your cheek into
your mouth.
Sadness feels like a wall that touches you as darkness arrives.
Sadness looks like a child doing daily chores in an empty
orphanage whilst wishing she was dead.
Sadness smells like a relation in hospital waiting for news of
their illness.
Sadness sounds like an animal whimpering in the darkness in
the jungle.
Sadness reminds me of grey clouds pouring with rain.

Amy Townshend (11)
Hill Top Primary School

Happiness

Happiness is like a bunch of freshly picked flowers.
Happiness is like having lots of warm showers.
Happiness reminds me of the bright yellow sun.
Happiness reminds me of a tasty cherry bun.

Happiness tastes like a breath of fresh air,
Happiness is full of lots of love and care.
Happiness sounds like wedding bells,
Happiness reminds me of summer smells.

Happiness feels like I could run a mile,
Happiness feels like when I smile.
Happiness smells like rose petals,
Happiness feels like when the snow settles.

Happiness is free!

Rebecca Willoughby (11)
Hill Top Primary School

Love

Love feels like your heart is on fire
And you own your own desire.

Love looks like a bunch of kittens,
While old ladies are knitting a pair of mittens.

Love reminds me of when my mum is hugging me
And when I am thinking of the sea.

Love sounds like a waterfall is splashing on the bottom of the fall
And drops of water are splashing on the side of a grey wall.

Love tastes like a big box of chocolates waiting at the door,
While a dog is giving you his paw.

Let's not forget love is everywhere,
Because love is in the air.

Lauren Wakelin (10)
Hill Top Primary School

Sadness

Sadness is grey, like a cloud raining over people, washing away
their happiness.

Sadness feels like the world is full of nastiness.

Sadness looks like a misty waterfall.
Sadness is like a devil's voice that calls.

Sadness reminds me of unfulfilled dreams,
Sadness is like a killing beam.

Sadness is when you need to heal,
Sadness is something that you feel.

Sadness is unhappiness!

Rebecca Bagley (10)
Hill Top Primary School

Fruit

Mangoes are as red as blood
They are as green as grass
They float away in the floods
And are softer than glass.

Apples are as red as autumn trees
And sour like a lime
Hard and smooth like icy peas
I eat them all the time.

Peaches are as yellow as the sun
Soft like a baby's head
They taste nicer than a bun
And are smaller than my bed.

Thomas Oakes (8)
Loxley Primary School

Sleeping

I am in my bed,
I cannot go to sleep,
I don't know why,
But then . . .

I fall asleep, I dream,
That I could sleep for ages,
That I never stop sleeping
And that I sleep forever.

Charlotte Bye (8)
Loxley Primary School

Sun Safety

If you are out in the sun
    You'd better get away,
You must stay in the shade
    And not get burnt today.

Remember your kids,
    Cook extremely quick,
Leave them out too long
    And they'll be very sick.

Megan Walker (9)
Loxley Primary School

Sleep

It was peaceful away
And I looked out at the bay,
The busy forest I'd seen
But now all was serene.

I lay there awake
And I looked at the lake,
The bed was so soft
As I looked out from my loft.

I remember what I saw
Upon the dark forest floor,
As I closed my eyes
The birds sang lullabies.

I was drifting off to sleep
In the forest so deep,
Dreams of wild rabbits
And all of their habits.

Natasha Moran (8)
Loxley Primary School

Fairy Skipping

I saw a fairy skipping one winter's afternoon,
The skipping rope as blue as the bluest sea,
With yellow stripes as blonde as a little girl's hair.

The fairy's wings as red as the reddest rose,
Her eyes as brown as the greatest tree's bark,
Whose leaves are as orange as a ginger cat.

The sun is as bright as the hottest fire,
The sky as blue as the deepest ocean,
And the grass as green as can be.

Iona McLeod (8)
Loxley Primary School

My Apple

The colour is as red as a rose, my apple.
Bite it and it makes a sound like a giant crunching bones, my apple.
The smell is like a tree on a crisp autumn day, my apple.
My apple, my apple, my apple.

It tastes as sweet as a summer's day, my apple.
It's really as juicy as the ripest mango, my apple.
The apple is as round as money so pay, my apple.
My apple, my apple, my apple.

My apple has a warm inside, my apple.
My mother said worms could live with their heads off, my mother.
The worm was half-eaten and I felt really sick, the worm.
My apple, my apple, my apple.

Cameron East (9)
Loxley Primary School

The Fruit Fairy

The fruit fairy was flying near houses the other day
And saw children going to school eating chocolate on the way.
She flew down and told them to eat fruit walking to school,
But they just ignored her and said she was a fool!

So off she went down to school while everyone was in class
And she silently fluttered through the big mass
Of lunch boxes and she peered inside and she saw,
Sweets and chocolate and candy galore!

So she swapped all the chocolate and sweets
With fruit and juice and healthy eats,
She did it every day and soon,
They loved fruit as much as the swimming pool!

Jasmine Blocksidge (9)
Loxley Primary School

Food

It feels like a water bomb,
It is as juicy as an apple pie,
You peel it like a potato,
What is it?

It feels like a smooth pebble,
It sounds like a bomb when you bite it,
You nibble it like a rabbit eats carrots,
What is it?

It feels like a bunch of marbles,
It tastes as squishy as a plum,
You pick it like a nit,
What is it?

Rebecca Weston (9)
Loxley Primary School

Apple

An apple is green
You can get one as large as a boat
It is as red as fire in my house
And it gets eaten by a mouse.

An apple grows on a tree
Bite it and it sounds like cornflakes going in the bowl
It looks rather like a huge piece of shiny coal.

Molly Smith (9)
Loxley Primary School

Do Exercises

If you want
To run like
Kelly Holmes
You don't want
To eat too many buns
Or damage your bones.

When someone
Is running
Out in the sun
Take care
Not to burn
Whilst out on a run.

If you like
To be
On the ball
When you
Get on it
Make sure you don't fall.

Harvey Hancock (9)
Loxley Primary School

Fruit

An apple is green,
Much bigger than a bean,
Soft like a cat,
But softer than a rat.

A lemon is as yellow as the sun,
A lemon is sour and that's no fun,
If you eat it too quick,
Be careful you're not sick!

Briony Davis (9)
Loxley Primary School

The Summer Fairy

There's a secret place I know
Where the summer fairy flies
Picking juicy, ripe fruit from golden orchards
And doing daring jumps so high.

The sun shone down
Upon the nearby town
All the children came out and clattered about
But some of the oldies frowned.

So go to the secret wood I know
Where the summer fairy plays
Hiding amongst the flowers
Fooling around all day.

There is a secret place I know
Where golden times are had
And the summer fairy eats ripe fruit all day
Oh my, she must be glad!

Jennifer Knowles (9)
Loxley Primary School

Health

Don't just sit and eat junk all day,
You should have fruit and go out to play.
If you don't run around,
You'll end up dead and buried under the ground.

If you want to be really fit,
You should go buy some running kit.
If you don't want to play outside,
You could learn to swim and dive.

Jack Sampson (8)
Loxley Primary School

Football

The feel of a football is like a rock,
As it whizzes past so fast,
The smell of a ball is so rubbery,
As you know you're the last.

You could score a goal,
The feel of a football is so nice,
Sometimes it's a really hard game or a game with pain,
The feel of a football in your hand is like ice.

When you spin the ball it might miss the goal,
When you think you've scored a goal the ref says no,
When you get the ball, have a go and score a goal,
When the ref blows his whistle, you will have to go.

Samuel Turner (8)
Loxley Primary School

Running Health

Running is like you're in a car
And you can run very far,
Go and buy your own running kit
And run around to stay fit.

Instead of sitting on the sofa all day,
You could go out and have a play.
If the sun has come out,
You could have a run about.

Go and have a run at the park,
You could run until it's dark.
Practise hard, you could win a race,
If you keep up with the pace.

Kieran Quick (9)
Loxley Primary School

Your Health

Don't just snack on sugar all day,
When you could go outside and play.
When you are playing outside,
It will help you keep alive.

Go and walk in the park,
With a dog who likes to bark.
Exercise well and you will see,
Just how healthy you can be.

Go outside and race your dad,
Even though you could get beat bad.
It's OK to have some sweets,
But it's better to eat meat.

Jake Chorlton (9)
Loxley Primary School

Fruit

Apples are as crunchy as a cereal bar
Apples are as red as a rose.
Bananas are as yellow as the sun
Bananas are soft when I eat them.

Oranges are orange like Lucozade
When I squeeze an orange
It looks like raindrops when juice comes out.
Pears are as green as a leaf.

Grapes are tasty food
Grapes are as sweet as a bird.
Peaches are as sweet as fruit juice to drink.

Sophie Barnsley (9)
Loxley Primary School

Flavours Galore

Water is as clear as glass
It sounds like the splashing ocean.
Water can be hot like a warm summer's day
Or cold as a winter's night.
Water glistens like a precious gem
It's refreshing as a mint.
Water feels smooth like a sheet of ice
And it freezes in a freezer.

Mark Raw (9)
Loxley Primary School

Anger

Anger is like the sunset at the end of the day
Anger feels like burning inside your heart
Anger sounds like a thunderstorm in your head
Anger reminds me of times I have been hurt
Anger looks like a murderer about to strike
Anger smells like smoke from a fire
Anger tastes horribly bitter.

Ben Sproston (8)
St Marie's Catholic Primary School, Sheffield

Love

Love feels like my heart is beating.
Love is red like a rose.
Love tastes like a chocolate cake.
Love looks like a big heart.
Love smells like a strawberry cake.
Love reminds me of a couple.
Love sounds like a violin.

Michelle Maora (8)
St Marie's Catholic Primary School, Sheffield

Fear

Fear is black like a lonesome, dark sky
It sounds like a scared child screaming
It feels like a strong, prickly tree
It looks like a big, dark shadow
It reminds me of a deep, gloomy hole
It tastes like a sour, bitter berry
It smells like a horrible garbage bin.

Tyler Simmonite-Scott (8)
St Marie's Catholic Primary School, Sheffield

Sadness

Sadness is black, like a deep dark cave in a deep dark wood.
Sadness feels like you're trapped in a dark prison cell
And there's no way out.
Sadness smells like gas coming nearer and nearer to you.
Sadness tastes like dark chocolate, bitter in your mouth.
Sadness looks like slimy goo, dribbling down on the floor.

Paris Dephley (9)
St Marie's Catholic Primary School, Sheffield

Sadness

Sadness is blue like a tear shed from your eye.
Sadness reminds me of the bad news of when my uncle Joe died.
It smells like the flowers at a funeral.
It feels like you've been run over by a car.
It sounds like a roar from a lion.
It looks like blood dripping from you.
It tastes like charcoal burning in your mouth.

Dominic Casey (9)
St Marie's Catholic Primary School, Sheffield

Anger

Anger is red like blood-red tomatoes.
It sounds like a heart pumping up and down.
It looks like horrible, mouldy food.
It feels like a surge of pain coming down your spine.
It tastes like gone-off toast.
It reminds me of when my great uncle Antony died.
It smells like burnt toast.

Jack Clohessy (9)
St Marie's Catholic Primary School, Sheffield

Love

Love is red like poppies swaying in the breeze.
Love feels like a big juicy apple.
Love looks like a huge red heart.
Love sounds like robins singing in a tree.
Love reminds me of my family.
Love is like a red sunset in the distance.
Love smells like a Sunday supper.
Love tastes like Christmas dinner.

John Rossiter (9)
St Marie's Catholic Primary School, Sheffield

Silence

Silence is yellow like halos on angels
Silence sounds like peace in Heaven
Silence feels like night-time sleep
Silence smells like blossoms in spring
Silence reminds me of silence in my room
Silence tastes like pineapple in my mouth
Silence looks like the shining of the sky.

Ophelia Phillips (8)
St Marie's Catholic Primary School, Sheffield

Hate

Hate is black like the darkness at night
It reminds me of fire burning a forest
It smells like smoke from a forest fire
It feels like hot, burning ashes
It tastes like overheated pancakes
It sounds like an evil laugh shouting
It looks like a big fireball ready to crash into a city.

Ian Mercado (9)
St Marie's Catholic Primary School, Sheffield

Silence

Silence is white, like the peace in Heaven,
It looks like the deserted desert,
It feels like a soft, fluffy cloud,
It smells like blossom in springtime,
It sounds like angels singing in harmony,
It tastes like a plain piece of bread with nothing on it,
Silence reminds me of the gates opening to Heaven.

Sophie Farrell (10)
St Marie's Catholic Primary School, Sheffield

Fun

Fun is yellow like a bright spring flower
Fun is like a bright yellow sun
Fun feels like happiness in the sky
Fun smells like strawberries and ice cream
Fun looks like children playing in the park
Fun reminds me of being happy!

Alex Kilcommons (9)
St Marie's Catholic Primary School, Sheffield

Anger

Anger is red like a burning hole in Hell
Anger smells like thick black smoke
Anger sounds like thunder and lightning
Anger feels unfair
Anger tastes like hot spice
Anger looks like red blood
Anger reminds me of evil spirits!

Fadzai Chitunhu (9)
St Marie's Catholic Primary School, Sheffield

Happiness

Happiness is bright yellow like a smiling face
Happiness looks like the sun shining
Happiness feels like running through a sunflower patch
Happiness smells like jasmine on a summer afternoon
Happiness reminds me of sitting on the beach
Happiness sounds like the laughing of a child
Happiness tastes like a triple layer chocolate cake.

Katherine Stent (10)
St Marie's Catholic Primary School, Sheffield

Love

Love is red like the rosy red rose
Love feels like the cool breeze of the wind
Love tastes like a lemon sorbet on a hot day at the beach
Love smells like lasagne with crusty cheese
Love reminds me of my neighbour
Love sounds like the peace of Heaven
Love looks like the blood of Jesus.

Owen Creaser-Smith (10)
St Marie's Catholic Primary School, Sheffield

Anger

Anger is red like the petals of a dark red rose
It feels like Krakatoa exploding inside me
It smells like hot ash spurting out fire
It tastes like burnt Sunday dinner in my mouth
It reminds me of a rocket taking off in my mind
It sounds like five hundred bombs going off at once
It looks like a murderer about to kill!

Chinyere Clarke (10)
St Marie's Catholic Primary School, Sheffield

Hate!

Hate is pitch-black like the dirty ground
Hate feels like dark black scorpions nipping at your face
Hate reminds me of dark black rain clouds in the summer holidays
Hate sounds like the dreadful screaming of someone in a
car accident
Hate smells like a smoky alley down town.

Kerry Dodds (10)
St Marie's Catholic Primary School, Sheffield

Hate

Hate is dark red like blood that drips on the ground into a puddle,
It sounds like the dripping of the tap, *drip-drop,*
It looks like blood running down until it stops,
It feels like hated black eyes staring at you,
It tastes like sour sweetness inside your mouth,
It smells like dangerous fire burning,
It reminds me of danger that is coming towards me!

Francesca Androsiglio (9)
St Marie's Catholic Primary School, Sheffield

Love

Love is pink, like blossom blowing in the wind.
It feels like ice cream melting in your mouth.
It sounds like romantic music swirling around your head.
It smells of apple blossom fresh on a tree.
It looks like a big balloon floating in the air.
It reminds me of a big, giant hug from my mum.

Annie Rowland (9)
St Marie's Catholic Primary School, Sheffield

Sadness

Sadness is blue like rain dripping from the sky.
Sadness sounds like the wind rustling through the trees.
Sadness smells like salt being washed away by the sea.
It sounds like water going underground.
It looks like a white flower falling in the sky.
It tastes like sour lemon melting in your mouth.

Wankumbu Chisala (9)
St Marie's Catholic Primary School, Sheffield

Love Is . . .

Love is pink,
Like blossom blowing in the air.

Love smells like strawberries
Growing in the garden.

Love sounds like your heart
Beating gently like soft drums.

Love looks like your soul
Hovering in your body.

Love reminds me of when I kiss my mum
Before I go to school.

Love feels like balloons
Flying in space.

Love tastes like beetroot
Lying in the ground.

Isaac McCaffrey (8)
St Marie's Catholic Primary School, Sheffield

Anger

Anger is red like fire
Burning in your face
It reminds me of lava
Burning in a volcano

It sounds like a motorbike
Revving really fast
It looks like a red devil
Burning in every place

It smells like a big barbecue
Melting on the tray
It tastes like hot sausages
Sinking in your mouth.

Brayden Fallon (9)
St Marie's Catholic Primary School, Sheffield

Happiness

Happiness is yellow like the sun
Gleaming happily in the sky.

It feels like the furry softness
Of a teddy smiling all day.

It reminds me of a roller coaster
Whizzing around the world!

It looks like a huge smiley face
Grinning in my eyes!

Happiness tastes like a mouth-watering chocolate cake
Melting in my mouth!

It smells like a giant chicken on the BBQ
Whiffing up my nose.

It sounds like laughs of joy
Giggling round my head.

Daniel Padfield (9)
St Marie's Catholic Primary School, Sheffield

Anger

Anger is red like fire
Burning in your eyes.

It feels like an earthquake
Shaking in your head.

It reminds me of lightning
Striking down my brain.

It tastes like fire
Burning in your mouth.

Anger sounds like a motorbike
Racing in your brain.

Anger looks like veins
Straining down your body.

Montelle Williams (8)
St Marie's Catholic Primary School, Sheffield

Happiness

Happiness is yellow like the sun
Glowing brightly in the sky.
It smells like cakes
Wafting in my nose.

It feels like a soft cushion,
Brushing past my skin.
It tastes like sugar,
As sweet as you can get.

It looks like children playing,
Happy and full of joy.
It reminds me of a smiley face
Winking happily.

Iman Syed (8)
St Marie's Catholic Primary School, Sheffield

Anger

Anger is red like a thorny rose
Pricking the fingers of love and compassion.

It looks like a blockage between us and God
Keeping us from love.

It tastes like acid
Melting your insides.

It sounds like an ancient storm
Raging on Saturn.

It feels like walking on spikes
Cutting your feet open.

Naomi Snelson (8)
St Marie's Catholic Primary School, Sheffield

Hate

Hate is green like warty toads,
Croaking by the pond.
Hate tastes like poison,
Churning your guts.
Hate looks like a trapped lion,
Roaring for freedom.
Hate sounds like the screeching of a banshee,
Wailing in the night.
Hate smells like rancid manure,
Swarming with flies.
Hate feels like a burning iron,
Pressed against your cheek.

Bethany Kirkbride (9)
St Marie's Catholic Primary School, Sheffield

Monster Poem

Scary, spooky monster crept up the stairs,
Scary, spooky monster smelt like a juicy pear.
Scary, spooky monster liked his straight hair,
Scary, spooky monster turned over there.
Scary, spooky monster had a very bad day,
Scary, spooky monster cheered goodnight
And in the sunny morning he'll have a big *fright!*

Megan Hamer (9)
Shafton Primary School

Aeroplane Poem

When I got onto the massive blue plane,
I really wanted my nana's pet great Dane.
Soon we were flying into the air,
I got travel sick and I was scared.

I jumped, I screamed,
I nearly broke the screen,
My ears went pop,
I nearly forgot to suck a lollipop.

I went to sleep on the plane,
It really wasn't the same,
I thought we were going to crash,
Then I felt a splash.

It was nearly the end of the trip,
I asked my mum if I could skip.
She whispered to me, 'No.'
I said, 'Oh no! It's going to snow.'

Emily Armitage (9)
Shafton Primary School

Monsters

Scary monsters frightening us,
Scary monsters all around us,
Scary monsters terrifying us,
Scary monsters spooking us,
Scary monsters with sharp teeth,
Scary monsters locking the doors,
Scary monsters giving me a fright,
Scary monsters in the night,
Scary monsters green and ugly,
What is this place?
I am getting scared,
I don't like these ghosts floating around.

Kyle Cooper (9)
Shafton Primary School

Go-Karting

Go-karting is rather scary,
But they don't call me a fairy!

Racing round the karting track,
Must be careful or I might splat!

Driving round the corners it is cool and fast
But slowing down and skidding is not for any old fool.

Adam Whittaker (9)
Shafton Primary School

My Special Friend

I have someone special
I would like you to meet
He is cute
He is cuddly
He is small
He has a smile that makes me happy.

Patch is his name
He was given by someone special
He is light when I pick him up
He has a smile that makes me happy.

He has never been dirty
He is always clean
I have never lost Patch
He has a smile that makes me happy.

Patch is cute as his brown eyes stare
His nose is black and tiny
He has a little smile that makes me happy.

His white paws
Small and furry
Don't make any noise
He has a smile that makes me happy.

His little white tail sways to and fro
His dark brown ears are floppy and soft
He has a smile that makes me happy.

Patch has two patched eyes
He has a brown and white body
That is furry, but smooth
He has a smile that makes me happy.

He's lovely, my Patch
I'm sure you would say that too
He has a smile that makes me happy.

Emma Chappell (11)
Shafton Primary School

Old Bear

My old bear's life is wearing out,
He's got to go
Mum says, without a doubt.
He's old and grey
And wants to be loved,
Everyone says I love you
And that's been proved.

I keep him close to me every night,
So old bear, don't get a fright.
He's gloomy and cold
With a snow-flaked nose.
They all say he's cute
And that's what he knows.

I feel lonely when he's not around,
He sleeps on my bed and makes no sound.
I keep thoughts of him
And cuddle him when I'm down,
When I'm sad I look at him and frown.

He means the world to me,
He's the bear that I want,
He gives me memories of my family
Who have died.
Forever, old bear will be by my side.

Alice Lockwood (11)
Shafton Primary School

The Millennium Stadium

The mighty roar of the Barnsley fans in the Millennium Stadium
As the players walked on the pitch, every word was clear.
I bet the opposition fans could hardly hear.

The echo of the noise rattled through the town,
I bet the vibration could have broken the prince's crown.

Red and white flags were flying everywhere,
One of the Swansea fans came into the Barnsley stand for a dare.

I think he was very, very worried,
If I were him I think I would have been buried.

Let's hope Barnsley FC win,
Or I'll be hiding in a tin.

Matthew Malloy (10)
Shafton Primary School

My Rosary

It's light when I gently lift it up
It's special to me
Each bead stands for a prayer
It's shiny and polished for me.

It's light when I gently lift it up
It's special to me
This gift I got is delicate
Smooth and beautiful for me.

I pray with it every night
I keep it in a safe place
It also helps me to remember God
And memories I had with it.

At my Confirmation
My friend gave me a 'well done' gift
On the 8th of December
I entered the life of Jesus.

This rosary brings back memories
Of when my family were there
Reminds me of my Confirmation
It was a great day.

This gift my friend gave me
Is cared for and loved
It's put in a special place
I hold it in my hand now.

Shannon Hatfield (10)
Shafton Primary School

Super Dog, Sam

It's smooth and gentle,
Funny and springy,
But absolutely mental,
Swims in a dinghy.

It's black and brown,
Soft and fluffy,
Can put on a frown,
And he's not puffy.

It's fast and healthy,
He won't stop running,
He could be wealthy,
He is really cunning.

It's huge and cuddly,
He runs up hills,
He runs round funnily,
He's got awesome skills.

Ashley Brownsword (11)
Shafton Primary School

Leo The Lion

It has black beady eyes
And black lengthy whiskers,
With a brown furry nose.
Its soft brown ears,
Stick out from its hair,
It's cuddly and furry
And always there.
Its brown, fat belly,
Has a small belly button,
That is smooth and brown.
On the back of him,
Hangs a long bushy tail
Bulging with fur.

I tell him my worries,
When I'm down in the dumps,
He helps me through bad times,
He's loving and caring.
He tells me stories,
Through our memories,
He's always there,
Waiting for me.

My lion was a gift,
From a special friend,
Who moved away
To a foreign land.
I haven't seen her since
She moved away,
But Leo the lion
Is here to stay.

Chloe Wilson (11)
Shafton Primary School

My Teddy Bear

Its black beady eyes stare at me as I cuddle it,
Its red and green bow tie makes it look cute,
Its little fluffy ears stick out of the top of its head,
Its big furry paws have tiny black claws sticking out of them,
Its small little nose just adds to the beauty of my teddy bear.

I cuddle it when I'm afraid,
It makes me feel special,
It's always there for me,
It's the first thing I see
As it sits at the end of my bed.

My teddy was a gift,
It's special to me,
I've had it since I was born,
I never met the person I got it from.

I love my teddy,
It loves me too.
I always know I will be with him,
My teddy bear.

Bethany Farrell (10)
Shafton Primary School

My Teddy

Its tiny ears on top of its head,
Listen as you talk,
Its feet aren't big and smelly,
I can't take it for a walk.

Its fluffy tail is like a bauble,
It has stitches on its face,
Its shirt says 'Happy birthday',
Squashed up in a case.

She sits on my television,
I cuddle her at night,
I think about the memories,
When I hold her tight.

I got her for my birthday,
From my best friend, Kate,
I think it's really special,
She'll always be my mate.

Katie Firth (11)
Shafton Primary School

My Dad

My dad is always happy,
When I am around,
I always cheer him up,
Without making a sound.

His dark brown eyes water,
As you look at him,
For the best dad in the world,
He should win.

His reddish coloured face,
Never gives a frown,
That's why he hasn't any wrinkles,
He deserves a crown.

He always looks smart,
When we're going out,
When he gets angry,
He doesn't shout.

The reason I love my dad,
Because he loves me,
When it is teatime,
He always makes my tea.

Rebecca Dawson (11)
Shafton Primary School

My Ted, Snowflake

It looks cuddly
Soft and squidgy
It makes you want to cuddle it
I look at him in the morning
And cuddle him at night
I make sure that he is safe
In all the morning light
Before I go to school
I lie him with his friends
He tells them all the rules
Did I mention
He is so cool?
I won't let anything happen to him
Because he is my teddy bear
I will always care
I will never get a new bear
I will pass it on
He can sing my children a song
I love him so much
Because he is my teddy bear.

Jordan Seres (11)
Shafton Primary School

My Rabbit

I cuddle my rabbit all night long
I feel safe when he comes along
I talk to him when I'm sad and lonely
His smile keeps me happy
He's my one and only.

His shaggy fur
His beady black eyes
Put you off rabbit pies
He looks at you
When you say your goodbyes
He never sighs
He never cries
When you look at his beady eyes.

I got him from Birmingham
Where I had some fun
Where I met my aunt's friend Pam
Where I was looking at her webcam.

He sits on my bed
As I scratch my head
He will never be dead
My little rabbit, Ted.

Heidi Walsh (10)
Shafton Primary School

My Golden Teddy Bear

I have a golden teddy bear
Its fur is silky and smooth
And every time I cuddle him
My memories are on the move.

It has a pink ribbon around its neck
And when I wake up I give it a peck.
Its dark black eyes sparkle in the night
And when I'm sad and lonely, I squeeze it tight.

This teddy means a lot to me as I love him so
My dad bought it just for me, I'll never let it go.
I keep it very close to me
I'll love it forever
I'll never have another teddy like you
That feels as soft as a feather.

Amy Merton (11)
Shafton Primary School

My Bear

My bear is big,
Soft and furry,
As brown as the bark on a tree,
A face as happy as mine,
A red and white ribbon makes him look smart,
He is as light and cute as a puppy,
As delicate as can be,
His ears stick up and a bit of pink
Makes him loveable to me.

Alex Hinchliffe (10)
Shafton Primary School

Oakwell From The Ground

Its vibrant colour,
Gets more lush and green as it grows,
The heavy winds blow, but still it stands,
It looks ever so grand,
It's very healthy,
I love it so, this beautiful land,
I'll never let go.

I glare at it madly,
I sometimes look at it sadly,
I leave it on my window sill to leave it to grow,
I have to give it water,
Or it would have to be slaughtered,
It brings back good memories of the day,
As I always dream about it as I lay.

It came from Oakwell,
It knows lots of old folks well,
I ran on the pitch as I looked like a witch,
As I picked it up, I had to duck,
It was a great day as I think about it and lay,
I went to the match and tried to get a bit of a patch.

I love this Oakwell grass,
It's very special to me,
It's only special because I picked it myself.
I love supporting the super Reds,
I love football, especially Barnsley FC,
It brings back the best memories of all,
It is Barnsley Football Club,
The pride of Yorkshire's grass.

Helena Crane (11)
Shafton Primary School

My Dog Piper

She is heavy,
Yes, it shows,
She gets bigger
As she grows.
She's cuddly and soft,
With big brown eyes,
She's liver and white,
She's never out of my sight.

Her ears are brown and floppy,
Her coat is soft and smooth,
She's always on the move,
So get ready to groove.

She always like to play with me,
I love her when she's there,
I always, always care for her,
I really love her hair.

Her name is Piper,
She is really cute,
I really love Piper,
I think that you would too.

Bethany Turner (11)
Shafton Primary School

My Teddy Bear

It's soft as I pick it up
And cuddly when I touch it,
It's as scruffy as a dog,
But brown as a cat.
It's small enough to carry,
But big enough to cuddle,
It has large black paws
And loveable fur.
It's very heavy,
But very smooth.

Jerome Harber (10)
Shafton Primary School

My Special Teddy

My special object is;
Soft like a feather when I pick it up,
Cuddly at night when I'm in bed,
It wears blue clothes all the time,
It has dull brown fur, fluffy and warm,
It looks happy and comfortable on my bed,
It is big enough to cuddle and small enough to take away.

James Wragg (10)
Shafton Primary School

Trophy

It's hard and smooth
And is as light as a feather
The sun shines on the glitter
When it's shiny and polished

I keep it in a cabinet
Nice and safe
As you look around
It is the first thing you see

I have achieved something
I have tried my best
There's nothing like winning
I am the best

As I look after it
And polish it clean
I remember how I got it
In the memories that I dream.

Charlotte Wignall (11)
Shafton Primary School

My Teddy

Smooth and small,
Happy and cuddly,
Short cream fur,
Big black eyes,
That's my teddy.

Jade got it for me
When I was on holiday,
He's friendly and kind,
Safe and cuddly,
That's my teddy.

He came from holiday,
From inside a grabber machine,
He reminds me of my dog,
That's my teddy.

Harry Wheatman (10)
Shafton Primary School

My Teddy Bear

Soft and cuddly,
Long blue fur,
Shiny black eyes,
That's my bear.

It was given to me
When I was born,
Dad got it for me,
It is lovely and friendly,
Just like me.

I feel safe when I'm around it,
It's the first thing I see,
I cuddle it more and more
And it cuddles me.

Connor Sagar (10)
Shafton Primary School

Fit Young Man Called Paul

There is a fit young man called Paul
Who wants to kick a football
But he will find it hard
To receive a red card
While he is only two feet tall.

Adam Lawson (10)
Shafton Primary School

My Dog

My dog is so cute and so small
He loves to go play with his ball
I love him loads and loads
Even though he eats toads
To him I must seem very tall.

Cally Strutt (10)
Shafton Primary School

There Once Was A Man From China

There once was a man from China
He thought he was a good climber
He slipped on a wet rock
And lost his big new sock
So now he's changed to a miner.

Bradley Bailey (9)
Shafton Primary School

England

England are a brilliant team
I hope that I'm not in a dream
I hope that we don't lose
Dad will drink lots of booze
And it will make my mother scream!

Jazmine Walker (10)
Shafton Primary School

School Dinners

School dinners are tasty and hot
Mushy peas look just like green snot
Potatoes are bumpy
The gravy's all lumpy
But I have to eat up the lot.

Kyle Taylor (10)
Shafton Primary School

10th Birthday

It is my 10th birthday today,
'Happy birthday,' said my friend Kay
I bought chocolate cake
I have to be awake
Today I will get my own way.

Bethany Wood (9)
Shafton Primary School

A Girl Called Kerry

There once was a girl called Kerry
Who always ate a strawberry
She had lots of good fun
In the bright yellow sun
She and her brother called Terry.

Alex Joburns (10)
Shafton Primary School

The Man From Spain

I know someone who went to Spain
On the way home he missed his plane
So he got very mad
And he hit a young lad
So he never went there again.

Rose Whitelam (10)
Shafton Primary School

Flowers

Flowing flowers along the beach
I can see them all
Light lilac colours
Which they all are
There will be more and more.

Flowing flowers along the beach
I can see them all
They look so beautiful
As they grow near the shore.

Flowing flowers along the beach
I can see them all
Waves wash over the delicate flowers
Their soft petals should have some more.

Flowing flowers along the beach
I can see them all
Will the lovely flowers be there
Or will they have gone?

Elizabeth Wignall (8)
Shafton Primary School

The Monster

Once there was a monster on the go,
He went into town and ate some dough.
He rushed and rushed to have a look around,
Then he ended up on the ground.

The monster was magic and had a wand,
He turned a man into a pond.
He looked at the magic trick he was doing,
The pond decided to give him a gluing.

The monster heard a noise,
The noise was only his toys.
His toys were squeezy and soft,
Even though they lived in the loft.

Bang, bang, bang! there was a knock at the door,
He had never heard a bang before.
It was only his monster friend,
He hopes the friendship will never end.

Holly Lockwood (9)
Shafton Primary School

Dancing Poem

My dancing feet
Dance to the beat
The music makes me move
Moving to the groove.

My feet were tapping
The audience clapping
I floated around the floor
The audience wanted more.

I just do my best
Trying to pass my test
I need a rest
I'm very tired from my dance.

Tabitha Finnerty (8)
Shafton Primary School

Beautiful Birds

Birds fly with the beautiful feathers trailing behind them
Birds are the most wonderful creatures around
Swans are the most beautiful birds in the world
Bluebirds are lovely singers
Parrots' feathers are wonderful colours
Falcons swoop down to catch their prey
They are one of the fastest birds in the world.

Corey Daley (9)
Shafton Primary School

My Brother Has Got A Motorbike

My brother has got a motorbike
He went on a really big hike
He was gone for a long, long time
And he didn't say bye
He was riding with his mate, Mike.

Kelly Gregory (10)
Shafton Primary School

Athletics

There once was a gymnast called Kay
She took all her lessons in May
Competitions she won
A friend said, 'Good luck, hun'
And the loud audience cried, 'Hey!'

Hannah Barker (10)
Shafton Primary School

Monsters

Scary, spooky, enormous, fierce monsters
Frightening and terrifying me.
Talking shadows on the wall.
Hearing smashed bottles on the floor
Outside my door.
I hear a large sound.
It's haunting me.
It's a horrifying, spooky *monster!*
Argh!
There it is, I can see it through the window.
It's heard me.
The monster is climbing up a ladder.
I'm frightened - it wants to eat me!

Molly Lee (8)
Shafton Primary School

Life Underwater

Underwater, I'm a diver,
Off I go, I'm the last survivor.

See some dolphins around a submarine,
It's the biggest sub you've ever seen.

Wow, a ray, they're an endangered type,
The coral too is yellow and ripe.

Lots of bubbles, big and blue,
I'll catch an angelfish for you.

I see some fish in a school,
It's cold down here in this cool lagoon.

Slimy seaweed, brown and green,
Down here miracles are to be seen.

A whale shark, the biggest kind,
It only eats the plankton it can find.

Becky Hirst (9)
Shafton Primary School

Swimming

I am very good at swimming
Across the pool I like skimming
I wear my swimming hat
I look just like a cat
Even when the lights are dimming.

Haydn Brownsword (9)
Shafton Primary School

Touring Cars

The Seat Leon going fast,
The BMW comes last,
The pit crew are the best,
They wear their special vests,
Seats are so very fast.

Danny Hibbert (10)
Shafton Primary School

The Giant Cat In The Street

Granny went downstairs
And she opened the door
As she got outside she heard a big, loud roar
She said to herself, 'What is that?'
So she put on her specs and said,
'Run, there's a huge cat!'

She went to her neighbour and said,
'Run, there's a giant cat!'
So she and her neighbour told everyone on the street
And they ended up running into Crystal Peaks.

Daisy Hope (8)
Totley All Saints CE (VA) Primary School

School Chaos

Hear pencils rattling
And children battling.
Hear teachers shouting
And parents bouting.
Hear children singing
And hear them dancing.
Hear children moaning
And teachers groaning.
Hear children panting
And hear them stamping.
All the children stuck on work
Why do teachers have to lurk?

Emmy Beeby (8)
Totley All Saints CE (VA) Primary School

Thank You Poem

Thank you for cooking
Thank you for cleaning
Thank you for putting me to bed at eight o'clock.

Thank you for playing
Thank you for helping
Thank you for taking me for a walk.

Thank you for loving
Thank you for shopping
Thank you for everything.
        Thanks a lot.

Katie Harvey (7)
Totley All Saints CE (VA) Primary School

My Dream Castle

My castle would be purple with a bit of pink
My castle would be big
My castle would have a big swimming pool
My castle would be shiny
My castle would be very, very clean
My castle would have a lot of servants
My castle would have a big squash court
My castle would have a big computer
My friends would come every night
My castle would have big rooms
My castle would have a stable with horses
What would your castle be like?

Mia Wilson (7)
Totley All Saints CE (VA) Primary School

At The Beach In Summer

At the beach in summer
I hear shouts and screams
Everybody wants to play with me.

I eat dripping ice cream
And swim in the sea
I sunbathe on the beach
Whilst I eat a dripping peach.

I make myself look cool
And I fish in a rock pool
But a crab gets my toe
And I say, 'Let go!'

I walk home feeling very nice
And then I'll eat a big choc ice!

Megan Jones (8)
Totley All Saints CE (VA) Primary School

God

Dear, dear God, He loves you and me,
He loves everyone,
He loves Jesus and all of us,
He gives love to everyone,
He gives love to Christians,
Every single church,
He gives us love every single day,
He gives us food every day,
He never stops giving,
He gives to kids.

Sam Smith (7)
Totley All Saints CE (VA) Primary School

The Wind Blows

The wind blows
River flows
Birds sing
Church bells ring
Teenagers kissing
Snakes hissing
Children lying
Workmen hiding
Doctors helping
Midwives groaning
Ladies trying
Babies crying.

Emily Hulme (8)
Totley All Saints CE (VA) Primary School

In The Forest

In the forest with lots of trees
The mud is splashing up your knees.

Squelch, squash, your feet sink down
In the unusual yucky brown.

Splash, splash in the quagmire river
The cold wind makes the trees shiver.

Slip, wobble, wobble,
Ooops!

Libby Honnor (8)
Totley All Saints CE (VA) Primary School

The Ghost Of The Past

A thousand years ago,
When the moon was shining on the Earth below,
A silent figure appeared in the fog,
The woods were chopped log by log,
Please children, do not draw near,
For even greater things that you may fear . . .

A noise shattered the peacefulness of the night,
Then far away a glowing light,
The ghost of the past,
Had surfaced at last,
Please children, do not draw near,
For even greater things that you may fear . . .

It disturbed anything that had been built
And in the morning blood had been spilt,
It did nothing to help the needy and the poor,
Soon after it disappeared into the Earth's core,
Please children, do not draw near,
For even greater things that you may fear . . .

The people rejoiced,
It was happiness that they voiced,
The ghost of the past,
Had vanished at last,
Please children, do not fear,
The ghost of the past will never reappear.

Sanaa Ghori (11)
Westways Primary School

Fractions

It's a maths test,
A very, very, very boring one.
The questions on fractions are the best,
I don't know any fractions, none.

¼, what is that?
Help, help, *help!*
1/3, what about the SAT?
Yelp, yelp, yelp!

2/6, ½, are they the same?
Or are they not?
Oh, the pain,
The whole lot.

Hannah James-Louwerse (11)
Westways Primary School

My Wacky Family

My mum is mad
My mum is sad
My mum loves cars
My mum loves Mars

My dad likes SATs
My dad likes mats
My dad is crazy
My dad is lazy

My bro is slow
My bro is low
My bro wants money
My bro wants honey

Now talking about my sister
She's as horrid as a *blister*
She makes me embarrassed
Because she's not *weird!*

Hannah Grafton (11)
Westways Primary School

Love Poem

Love is like a rose,
Love is like a flower,
Love can change you,
You can cry, shout or laugh from love.

There's love between two,
There's love between families,
There's love all around the world
That won't ever end.

Loma Al-Dahiyat (10)
Westways Primary School

When I Become Ruler Of Coventry

Because it was ruined once, then twice,
The city turned from fire to ice.
I would have the city flooded,
The old cathedral would be put to rights.
The city turned from fire to ice,
Turned by dark and silver knights.
The old cathedral would be put to rights.
Planes will land and fly,
Turned by dark and silver knights,
Between the roads and sky.
Planes will land and fly,
All the city's evilness is hooded,
Between the roads and sky.
Birds wing in a wild way,
All the city's evilness is hooded,
Within that lake in one whole day.
Birds wing in a wild way,
I would have the city flooded,
Within that lake in one whole day,
Because it was ruined once, then twice.

Isaac Proudfoot (11)
Westways Primary School

Quest

Rushing through a winter's night,
I thought about my quest,
On the back of an ebony horse,
I had no time to rest.

To fight a mighty dragon,
To find the crystal staff,
To accept this almighty mission,
He must have been daft.

Through the fields of vicious battle,
He traipses carrying a mighty burden.

No one can see,
No one can know,
What a terrible fate,
Awaits our hero.

But now as the day draws to a close,
He has completed his task of which no one can know!

Meg Plowright (10)
Westways Primary School

My Granny's Pie

Jam, custard, tomato spread,
Butter, beans and some brown bread.
Salt, pepper, piggy thigh,
This is in my granny's pie!

Meat, steak, gravy too,
Ketchup, mustard, mixed to goo!
Peas, potato, a real delight,
I can't wait for dinner tonight!

The final ingredients,
(The last of obedience!)
Let's put in green dye,
In my granny's pie!

Joëlle Brabban (11)
Westways Primary School

The Craziest School On Earth

Our school, Splodgeways Primary,
Is really quite weird,
All across the country,
It's talked about and feared.

Our teacher's off his rocker,
He constantly screams and bellows,
His legs are short and plump
And his face is ghostly yellow.

Our hall is even stranger,
The ceiling's made of plastic,
We keep on bouncing up and down,
Cos the floor is all elastic.

'You seriously need more playtime'
The Ofsted inspector reckons,
And indeed this is too true -
It only lasts two seconds!

For our last school picture,
The teacher yelled, 'Pick your nose!'
Our photos looked disgusting,
As we sat gurning in rows.

You could explore London, Hong Kong or Rome,
Paris, Cape Town or Perth,
But I bet you'd never find *anything* like
The craziest school on Earth!

Rory Hanna (10)
Westways Primary School

Something That Is Breakable

In the forest I lie. In the sea I take my time.
There is no knowing where I shall be.
Up here and down there, everywhere you see me.
I am the great wave; I am the sun,
I am the evening star and the hare that runs.
I may not be visible; I may be silent.
I have the power to destroy or kill.
I have the power to rise and heal.
If I am gone there shall be no life.
If I am here everything lives.
The only thing I fear is the dreaded cold.
I wither and I melt and have no glow.
And when time has done her work, tired, old and aged,
I still go on.
I am still there.
I am watching you.
Every step of your life.

Woo-Jeong Yoon (11)
Westways Primary School

The Homework Monster

We hate tHis dreadful beast,
It gives us hOmework non-stop,
We like hiM the least,
We should sEnd out a cop,
They'd Win him of course,
He lOves gorse,
He Rocks with his girlfriend,
Kites he loves flying.

Milk he loves frying,
They Orbit the planet,
GiviNg out homework,
They Still get money
InsTead of honey,
Even though,
It's ouR teacher!

Rowan Drury   (10)
Westways Primary School